GW00730151

Occupied Behind Barbed Wire

By Gillian Carr

*In memory of all Channel Islanders who were
deported during the Occupation*

'In a prison camp the onslaught of boredom and depression is far more powerful and more serious in its effects ... The prisoners must rely largely on their own ingenuity and resources to keep their minds occupied and active.'

Prisoner of War: The first authentic account of the lives of British prisoners of war in enemy hands. Published by Horace Marshall and Sons Ltd, London (1942, 13).

'Father Christmas appeared at Biberach, to the great delight of the Channel Islands children. "I was up till 3 a.m. creeping about in my socks," he says, and his presents were no less than 180 toys made by himself and two others out of the inevitable Red Cross boxes and tins, using mainly a penknife and bits of glass. "I had managed to get the essentials for a handicrafts class from Guernsey, and the boys were very keen. The evening before, we had an exhibition, and it really was amazing to see the racing and armoured cars, lorries, gunloads, a battleship complete with several gun turrets, and tin guns, aeroplanes, etc."

The Prisoner of War magazine (April 1944, 14).

Occupied Behind Barbed Wire

By Gillian Carr

Contents

1

1

Background to deportations

Somewhat improbably, the reason for the deportations of Channel Islanders during the Occupation lies in the Middle East.

The reason for this was that in the summer of 1941, the war had spread to North Africa and the Middle East and both sides were struggling for control of that region's massive oil supplies. At the outbreak of war the Shah of Persia (as Iran was then called) was an open admirer of some of Hitler's policies and Germany was his country's main trading partner. By August 1941, Britain had already taken control of Iraq, feared that the Shah would renounce his neutrality and come out in favour of the Axis powers, and so, with their Russian allies, invaded Persia to secure the region.

That autumn, the British began to intern hundreds of Germans. Outraged, Hitler demanded that for every German citizen interned, ten British citizens resident in the occupied Channel Islands should be deported to the Pripet Marshes in Russia. Lists of Islanders were drawn up which were then lost in the bureaucracy of government as they were passed from department to department. The matter was brought back to Hitler's attention in September 1942, during a Swiss Government attempt to organise a prisoners of war exchange. He ordered an immediate evacuation of non-native Channel Islanders and within days, newspapers in the Islands published announcements describing the categories to be deported. Hundreds of Channel Islanders (men aged between 16 and 70) and their dependents, who included pregnant women and babies, were served with deportation orders. Being married to Island-born wives offered no security; indeed, some Island girls married their English boyfriends (and vice versa) at the eleventh hour to avoid being separated, even if it meant deportation to (and a honeymoon in) Germany. Many people had less than 12 hours to tie up their affairs, sell or give away the contents of their houses, put down or otherwise dispose of their family pets, deposit valuables and money with banks and arrive at the harbour with their families. It was a profoundly shocking and traumatic experience for those involved, and caused a great deal of resentment and hatred towards the occupying forces for those who were left behind. Many expressed their feelings by taking part in illegal demonstrations against the deportations, which, for some, led to prison sentences and future deportation.

The deportation document stated that people were allowed to take with them warm clothes, strong boots, meal dishes, a drinking bowl and a blanket. They were also allowed to pack a trunk of clothes, which would be sent on after them. For the most part, these were eventually to arrive safely in Germany against all expectations. Some exemptions were granted to people on the grounds of ill health or employment in essential services, but other people in this category were included in the second wave of deportations, which took place in February of the following year. This group of people included those who had 'offended against the German regime', and other 'undesirables' such as former officers who had served in WWI, Jewish people, high-ranking Freemasons, as well as some people from Sark, chosen in retaliation for a British commando raid which took place on the island in October 1942.

3

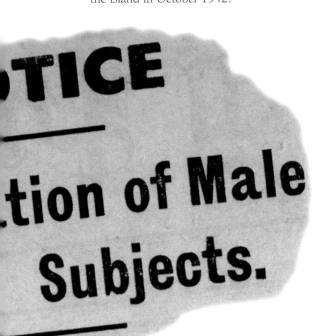

Watercolours showing deportation route through Europe.

The first deportees from Guernsey, and a few from Jersey (the rest of whom were otherwise sent straight to the camp in Biberach, southern Germany), were sent via the filthy, overcrowded and primitive transit camp of Dorsten, in the German industrial region of the Ruhr. The camp was a barrack-block style former PoW camp, and was so awful that it was considered by the men to be unsuitable to house their women and children. They stayed here for seven weeks, although the single men were sent to the camp in Laufen in south-east Germany after six weeks.

On 13 November 1942, the remaining Dorsten contingent arrived in Biberach (also a barrack-block former PoW camp) where they were greeted by deportees who had been sent straight there from Jersey. At about the same time as the single men from Dorsten were sent to Laufen, the single Jersey men in Biberach were also sent there. By the end of October 1942, many Jersey couples in Biberach, especially those with children, started to be moved to the nearby camp of Schloss Wurzach, leaving Biberach filled with mostly Guernsey internees. Although those in Wurzach were lucky to be all under one roof, first impressions of the camp were not favourable. Preston John Doughty from Jersey recorded in his diary that the day they arrived *'…will be remembered as long as we live, for the state of the place and our rooms were like pigsties and so everywhere we went, tears began to flow … Scrubbing of floors, doors, tables, chairs and, in fact, the whole place was undertaken to make it a fit place to live in. My room was like a large barn, and in it they put 46 men to eat and sleep. My wife was lucky for in her room they put 23 women, but it was to my mind the best in the camp.'* [1] Recalling his first experience of Wurzach, Michael Ginns remarked that *'the beds were damp, the place was filthy, but the British spirit prevailed and tables were scraped with broken glass and floors were scrubbed with half bricks and it was knocked into a semblance of order.'* [2]

The smaller group deported in February 1943 also travelled by boat to St Malo and were then herded onto a train. From the start, the women, children and men over 64 were sent to the rear of the train, and the younger men to the front. During the journey, and with enough warning time only to pull the men's possessions out of their wives' suitcases, the train split and the younger men, many of whom had wives in the back of the train, were taken on to Laufen and Kreuzburg; while the rest of the party travelled to Compiègne, just outside Paris. This was a barrack-block transit camp that held thousands of French Jews who were awaiting departure to concentration camps where most would die. The Channel Islanders, in a different part of the camp, saw them through the barbed wire. Like Dorsten, Compiègne was lice-ridden, filthy and overcrowded and the food was similarly meagre. By a stroke of luck, those arriving in the camp were helped by four American men who had been deported from Jersey when America entered the war. On learning that their former fellow Islanders were due to arrive in a neighbouring part of the camp, they did what they could to clean it up and provide mint tea for the new arrivals. These men were also able to organise things so that their Red Cross parcels could now and again be smuggled past the barbed wire and into the barracks where Islanders were placed for three months. On 21 May 1943, the Islanders were then sent on to Biberach. The men in Laufen with families in Biberach were allowed to join them in August 1943.

Although, in the beginning, everyday life within the camp was much constrained by roll calls, new German orders, fear, worry and hunger, soon people began to settle into camp life. The future stretched ahead of them, seemingly without end. Although many assumed or hoped that the Allies would win the war, there was no certainty when or if this would happen, and time rapidly began to weigh heavily on their hands.

Pen and ink sketch by Ernest Whiting of camp officers at Wurzach)

Deportees soon organised themselves, appointed a camp captain and various officers and organised the rest of the camp into a series of roles, duties, groups and fatigues. After a lot of hard work, tears and many months, the internees began to accept their new circumstances.

In total, some 2,200 people were deported from the Channel Islands. Precise numbers over time in each camp varied due to transfers between camps, births and deaths. Published records are incomplete, as are many unpublished official and unofficial camp registers (where they exist). Records are spread between a number of archives and private collections in the Islands today, which makes the task of exact accounting difficult. We have some precise figures taken by the Red Cross at certain points during internment, for example, in January 1943, 1,011 people were recorded in Biberach and 618 in Wurzach. In April 1944, there were 417 Channel Island men in Laufen, a camp that also held Americans. Other camps included Kreuzburg, Spittal/Drau and Liebenau, a camp for single women close to Biberach and Wurzach. Situated in an old castle, Liebenau shared premises with mentally disabled people who were looked after by nuns.

Biberach

Upper Square and Clock Tower House.
Biberach Camp.. Germany.

Laufen

Wurzach

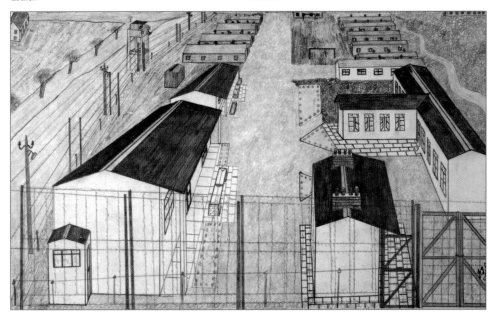

Dorston

Neither those left behind in the Islands, nor the deportees themselves, knew where they were being taken. By September 1942, people in the Channel Islands had already begun to hear rumours about concentration camps, as shown by entries in Occupation diaries. They knew such places existed, but did not know the horrors of what went on within them. Rumours circulated as they left the Islands. The deportees wondered whether they were going to be sent to their deaths or perhaps rescued by the Royal Navy, whom they hoped might be waiting for them in the Gulf of St Malo. Those left behind in the Islands also conjectured agonisingly about where their friends had been taken. In the event, letters arrived back in the Islands in early November. The deportees were able to reassure their friends that they were safe and being held in civilian internment camps. Leslie Sinel records in his Jersey Occupation diary that a batch of letters, probably written in Laufen, reached Jersey in early December 1942. More letters arrived in early January, and he records that *'these in the main are pathetic to read, for all appeal for food and warm clothing.'* [3]

Despite the long time-delay in their arrival, the brevity and the official censorship of these *Kriegsgefangenenpost* (POW) letter-forms and postcards, the emotions of the deportees and the events of their time in internment are still accessible to us today. The information in letters has been supplemented by those published by friends and relatives of deportees in the 'letters to the editor' section of the *Channel Islands Monthly Review,* a journal published by Channel Island refugees in the UK. We also have published and unpublished personal diaries and memoirs, such as those by Joan Coles, Mike Shepherd and Preston John Doughty in Wurzach, Edna Dorrian in Biberach, and Gerald Webb, Leslie Green and Frank Stroobant, who were interned in Laufen. Recent oral testimony has also been used to gather more information about events in the camps; the Guernsey Deportee Association and former members of the Jersey ex-Internee Association have been very helpful in this regard. These sources of information have together been used to understand the trauma of deportation as well as everyday life during the years of internment. **Sometimes, however, the most poignant tales are told by the artwork and handicrafts made by internees, which are today spread across private and public museums, archives and homes across the Channel Islands, and it is these that are the subject of this catalogue and the associated museum exhibition.**

2

Food and the Red Cross

From 12 December 1942 onwards, the Red Cross began to send regular parcels to the camps. People were so hungry that one internee wrote that she 'nearly ate the wrappings as well.' [4] Each person had to be individually registered before they could receive a parcel. These were very gratefully received by the internees who were living on German rations which consisted of thin and watery soup, sometimes-rotten potatoes, often-mouldy, black, dry rye bread [5], fish that was sometimes maggoty [6] (the taste of which was believed to be improved by frying), and substitute coffee or herbal tea that was so unpleasant to drink that the internees preferred to use it to clean tables, wash the dishes or fill hot water bottles. Internees continued to receive German rations throughout their time in the camps, even after the arrival of Red Cross parcels.

Descriptions of food and hunger dominate the diaries and memoirs of those interned. Joan Coles, when in Biberach, recorded how people were so hungry that they baked and ate potato peelings. [7] Eric Sirett said later that it was 'impossible to describe the misery caused by a combination of intense cold and malnutrition; it has to be experienced.' [8] This obsession with food is reflected in the artwork produced at

the time. Many images depict bowls of soup or dreams of better food in better times and locations, i.e. preferably back home.

Occupied Behind Barbed Wire

Despite the universal loathing with which the internees regarded the mouldy bread, they were so hungry that they ate it. In his Laufen memoirs, Leslie Green records that 'each loaf had to be divided daily into five ... *To make it as even as possible, he [the bread-cutter] would measure the bread with a ruler and mark it with a pencil. Everyone would watch, making sure each cut was vertical and shouting and swearing at him if they thought it was not. It was a thankless job. At the end would there be a mad rush for whatever pieces looked bigger.'* [9]

While still in Dorsten, Eric Sirett recalled that, one day, the Germans confiscated all bread knives, including his own, on the handle of which he had engraved his surname.

Eric Sirett's bread knife

Without a knife, it was impossible to cut the bread, so the next day, while reconnoitring the camp, he spotted a German guard through a window, labelling and recording the knives. While he watched, someone called the guard out of the room, so Eric reached in, found and retrieved his knife, and 'liberated' it. [10]

The soup queue - before and after!

The watery German soup was a source of grim amusement to the internees at Biberach and Wurzach. Despite their poor diet, they kept their sense of humour as shown by a sketch which shows the identification of four different types of soup. Red cabbage soup was called 'Blue Danube', white cabbage soup was called 'White Wings' because of the leaves of cabbage floating in it. 'Black Forest Soup' (millet soup) was so called because of the bits of husks and foliage that floated on the top, and swede soup was known as 'Golden Glory'. Queuing for this soup was a feature of everyday life in Biberach, as shown in the sketch above by Harold Hepburn. He also depicted the consequences of the endless diet of watery soup and black German bread: further queuing, but this time for the toilets. Even in difficult circumstances, the internees were able to smile at their circumstances.

Letters to Guernsey from Lillian and Jack Cannon in Biberach described how they ate *'mostly out of soup bowls and tins with soup spoons – knives and forks are not in great demand.'* [11] It seems that this was the impetus behind the carving of wooden eating implements, such as the spoon made by George Norman as a child, out of a Red Cross packing case .

Eric Sirett carved a utensil that had a spoon on one end and a fork on the other – just right for fishing things out of a Red Cross food tin.

Typical weekly menu of German rations at Biberach preserved in the archives of the German Occupation Museum in Guernsey:

Monday: Midday: swede and potato soup. Evening: maize and potato soup. 3 boiled potatoes, margarine and ⅕ loaf.

Tuesday: Midday: potato and cabbage soup. Evening: swede and water soup, 3 boiled potatoes, jam, ⅕ loaf.

Wednesday: Midday: fish goulash. Evening: potato and swede soup, 3 boiled potatoes, margarine, cheese and ⅕ loaf.

Thursday: Midday: sauerkraut and potatoes. Evening: swede and water soup, 3 boiled potatoes, jam and ⅕ loaf.

Friday: Midday: swede and potato soup. Evening: potato and maize soup, 3 boiled potatoes, margarine, fish cake and ⅕ loaf.

Saturday: Midday: cabbage and potato soup. Evening: no soup, 3 boiled potatoes, jam and ⅕ loaf.

Sunday: Sauerkraut, meat, gravy and potatoes. Evening: no soup, margarine, jam, cheese and ⅕ loaf.
Daily: Two mugs of mint tea each morning for breakfast.

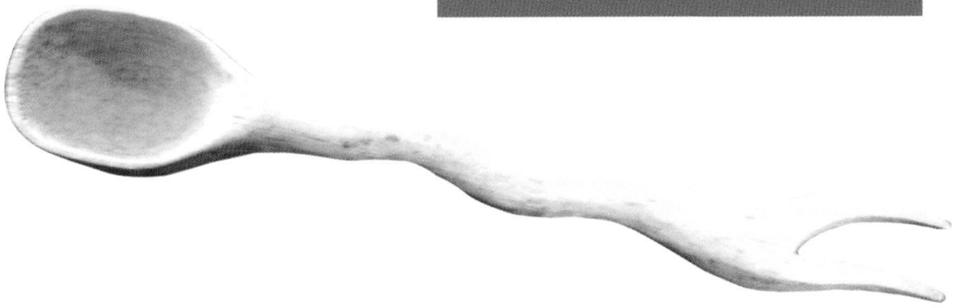

People also expressed their dissatisfaction with the food in verse. The following are by Eric Sirett and were composed in Biberach:

Sauerkraut
Is out
Of favour
By reason of its flavour
Or lack of it.

The German bread
That we are fed
On tastes like sawdust
Mildew-ed

I think
No other cheese
Can stink
Like these

The arrival of the Red Cross parcels caused great joy in the camps. They improved the general physical and mental health of the internees, who had begun to suffer the ill-effects of malnutrition and depression. Michael Ginns recalls that in Wurzach, after the arrival of the parcels, '*you could feel the tension, the depression, lift off the camp.*' [12] However, despite the arrival of the tinned food, the health of many internees continued to suffer due to the lack of fresh fruit and vegetables, which caused a lowering of the immune system. Diary entries recorded endless successions of colds, sore throats and coughs, which passed quickly through the camp. Several diarists recorded cutting their hands on the sharp edges of food tins. Such cuts often became infected and turned septic, needing frequent trips to the local hospital, and took a long time to heal. In April 1943, Jack and Lillian Cannon in Biberach wrote to Guernsey to ask if dried herbs could be sent to them to 'help their blood', as a fellow internee in the camp had to have two fingers and part of his right hand removed after getting a tiny scratch that got infected. [13]

Although the Red Cross and YMCA played an important role in supplying the internees with food and various materials, it is also clear that friends and family in the UK and in the Channel Islands were of great help to deportees; they could send next-of-kin parcels via the Red Cross, which were subject to various restrictions about what could be sent. Next-of-kin parcels were also sent from the Channel Island Refugees Committee. On 23 November 1943, for example, Gerald

Webb records in his Laufen diary that he *'received 50 cigarettes, a gift from the British Red Cross. Received a very much appreciated next of kin parcel as a gift from the Channel Islands Refugees Committee, London. It left the depot on October 4th and I received it today, just over 9 weeks travelling; very fast going. Contents of parcel was pair of shoes, pair of trousers, pair of socks, 1 vest, 1 scarf, 1 towel, 1 jacket, 1lb of chocolate, 1 bar soap, 1 stick shaving soap, 1 tin tooth powder.'*

Before the food situation became too desperate in the Channel Islands, some Islanders were able to send dried herbs, onions, beans, under-ripe fruit and vegetables to deported friends and family. Fresh fruit and vegetables were always very gratefully received as they provided a welcome and health-boosting change from the tinned food and German soup that was their normal fare.

Packets of real tea were a welcome item in Red Cross parcels. Internees in a room often donated a teaspoon of tea to the large communal jugs, which were then filled with hot water from the kitchens so that everyone could have a cuppa at mealtimes. Alternatively they could make their own private pot

using 'Klim' tins converted into teapots ('Klim', 'milk' spelled backwards, was a powdered milk product that came in Canadian Red Cross parcels). A few internees brought their own traditional Guernsey cans to Biberach; others made them, or else had them posted in next-of-kin parcels to use as teapots. Jack and Lillian Cannon wrote back to Guernsey that *'the Guernsey can is our most treasured possession. Jack had it embossed with our name and place of residence. This is necessary as all are potential thieves in this camp.'* [14] Hay-boxes were also made in Biberach to help keep drinks warm. [15]

Guernsey can engraved in Biberach

13

Because most of the food in Red Cross parcels came in tins, these soon began to pile up within the camp grounds and would smell bad in warm weather. We know that one of the regular fatigues (or jobs) of internees at Wurzach (and, most likely, the other camps) was to crush the tins and remove them from camp grounds, so that they would not prove a health hazard. Mike Shepherd's internment diary records how, on 5 May 1943, he spent five hours shovelling empty tins into a railway wagon. Later on, he wrote, *'as you can imagine, with everyone receiving a Red Cross parcel each week, empty tins soon accumulated and naturally took up much room. So this new fatigue entailed quite a dirty mess, because … most of* *the tins had some remains in them and when we began squashing them, meat, soup and what have you flew all over the place. Sometimes, if we hit a bad one, the smell was terrific.'* [16]

A few pictures taken after the liberation of Biberach show the pile of tins that built up in this camp at the end of the war; some internees still remember the smell and swarm of wasps that were attracted to the scraps of decaying food. The situation in Germany was very bad at the time and transport was badly affected, so the tins would not have been taken away.

Pile of Red Cross tins in Biberach after German rubbish removal carts stopped coming in 1945.

Courtesy of Peter Sirett

Recycling steel tins

Boredom was the key enemy of all internees. Because this could soon lead to depression, it was important to find a way to pass the time and distract thoughts. Letter and diary writing was popular but it didn't consume much time, and paper was often scarce, so other forms of activity were necessary. While we know that the Red Cross published a leaflet about recycling food tins in order to make useful items, we do not know whether the Islanders ever received this. The tins were especially easy and popular to recycle, once it was discovered that they could be easily flattened and folded or cut into new objects. Sharp ends could be folded over, edges could be crimped and surfaces could be and were engraved. People began to make plates, mugs and trays, sometimes engraved, and would give them as gifts. This became especially popular once the kitchenware brought from the Channel Islands began to wear out or break. Although this recycling work could be done, with some difficulty, without tools, the Biberach camp captain, Garfield Garland, was allowed to send a request to the Bailiff of Guernsey for a variety of carpentry and woodworking tools which were urgently needed. An advertisement was placed in the Guernsey Press and, on 10 November 1943, the tools arrived in the camp. The Germans insisted on keeping them under lock and key at night in case they aided escape or were used as weapons against the guards, but otherwise, they were kept in the camp workshop.

Some camp inmates made water heaters or primitive kettles out of large tins such as the Klim tin. In Wurzach, Frederick McAllister turned Klim tins into teapots. A plumber by trade, he used to visit the local plumber in the town, who gave him the solder and materials to make the spout and handles.[17]

Courtesy of Peter Sirett

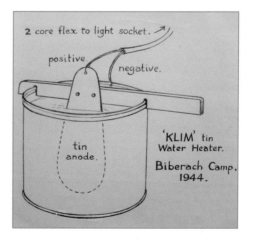

15

Other people made a range of different items out of tins, each of which reflected the different ways in which they chose to pass the time in the camp. Examples include sports trophies, hair curlers, and a communion chalice. This latter item was made in Biberach by 'Monty' Manning, and engraved with the phrase *'Ye that do truly and earnestly repent.'* Religious services were held in all camps, and several ordained ministers from a number of denominations were among the deported.

Many functional items were made out of recycled tins. In the Channel Island Monthly Review, a letter by Mrs J.F. Brittain was forwarded and published in which she wrote that *'a butter tin with fine holes in the bottom covered by a handkerchief, held in place with elastic, serves us for a coffee percolator; the bottom half is a Canadian milk tin. All our plates are made of biscuit tin.'* [18] In his internment diary, Preston Doughty describes making a primus stove to be independent of German supplies: *'When we got short of coal, a new idea was introduced into the camp. We have plenty of spare fat or margarine, so with this we began to be independent of the Germans. The fat was placed in a tin with the lid on the top; a hole was made in the lid, and a piece of string passed through, this tin being placed inside a much bigger tin with holes in the sides, and two pieces of tin used to prevent the receptacle from resting on the flame. It became one of the best of primus stoves!'* [19]

Mugs were sometimes made from empty Red Cross tins by folding down the sharp edges to prevent cuts. However, the most beautiful mugs to come out of Biberach were those engraved by Guernseyman Byll Balcombe. Although their origin is disputed, it is likely that these mugs had been left behind by the *Wehrmacht* (German army), who guarded the camps when the internees first arrived. In December 1942, these soldiers were replaced by the *Schutzpolizei* (German civilian police). Typically, these were older men – veterans of WWI. Some had even spent time in British PoW camps. Having been well-treated, they repaid the favour and showed kindness towards the deportees. On the whole, deportees got on well with their guards and, in several camps, good working relations were established with the odd bribe of cigarettes or chocolate from Red Cross parcels.

When the *Wehrmacht* were still in charge of Biberach, they had a store of metal kitchenware, which included mugs. It seems that one of the German Red Cross nurses brought some of these into camp for the deportees, although the reason for this is unknown. Several found their way to Byll Balcombe, who was skilled in metal engraving. Today, 15 engraved items by Balcombe have been recorded, and each one gives an insight into conditions in the camp and the preoccupations of the interned. Former deportees who were given mugs as children were told that he engraved them using a broken knitting needle and an old nail. In addition to engraving mugs, Balcombe also engraved one teapot and one shell case. The engraving of the shell case is significant; Balcombe fought in the trenches in the First World War and the art of engraving shell cases was a popular pastime for soldiers. It is likely that he learned his skill at this time.

Mug engraved by Byll Balcombe, showing the Wieland Linde.

William ('Byll') Balcombe

William John Balcombe was born in Suffolk on 28th September 1891. Although it is not known when he arrived in Guernsey, he joined the Royal Guernsey Artillery in around 1908. In January 1917 he married his sweetheart, Edith Beard. He had written to Edith throughout his army career and until his retirement in January 1919. This correspondence confirms that Balcombe saw active service in the Somme during WWI. His undisputed proficiency in 'trench art' suggests that he first learned this skill in the trenches of WWI, where the practice of engraving shell cases was a popular pastime for soldiers. Trench art are objects made by soldiers from material such as, often recycled, military hardware, shell cases for example, in a time of war. Aged 51 at the time of his deportation to Germany with Edith, Balcombe was employed as a house decorator (which is how he is described in his wartime ID card), although the camp register at Biberach describes him as a bookseller.

Balcombe's mugs are a rich source of imagery associated with internment, and all were turned into gifts (probably paid for with cigarettes, which often formed an alternative camp currency) to mark a special occasion. Several are christening mugs and others mark occasions such as Easter, births or wedding anniversaries. Some were simply used as thank you presents. Many depict the view just beyond the barbed wire at Biberach, the central image of which was the Wieland Linde, a linden tree planted to mark the engagement of Christophe Martin Wieland, a Biberachian writer and poet, in the 18th century. This tree, the farm buildings and landscape around it also occur in several paintings and drawings done in the camp by other internees. Balcombe often used this tree to symbolise love, and incorporated it in mugs engraved to commemorate wedding anniversaries. The inclusion of images of barbed wire on many mugs shows us his frustration at being interned and unable to wander about at will beyond the camp. Byll Balcombe is an excellent example of a phenomenon which was often seen in internment or POW camps, including those which contained Channel Islanders: an ordinary man whose artistic talents were, perhaps, unknown before internment, but which were able to be fully realised during this period of his life.

3

Women's camp fashion

Women often made bags, hats, belts, purses and other items of female fashion in camp. Food tins were cut up and folded to make rudimentary hair curlers It was a point of

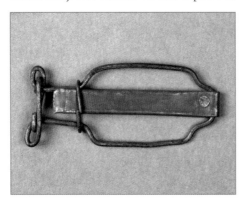

pride for the women to look smart. This was probably for the benefit of their men-folk, but was also part of keeping up appearances to boost morale. Looking smart was a challenge, as most people had a small supply of clothes that they had brought with them, and these were rarely suitable for all-season German weather.

The Red Cross would, from time to time, send consignments of old or second-hand clothes to the camps which were greatly appreciated by the internees. Some still remember today the old-fashioned nature of some of these.[20] On one occasion, a Hollywood props department sent a load of unwanted costumes to Laufen and one man received a gangster outfit![21] Whatever the

style of the clothes, they were all gratefully received, as the winter weather in southern Germany was particularly cold, and the number of 'briquettes' given to the internees as fuel for the stoves were notoriously insufficient in number. Many of the clothes sent were modified and adapted by the women to fit members of their family. Old or frayed woollen jumpers were unravelled, the wool washed, and the garments re-knitted. Worn out adult clothes were either turned into outfits for children, or else were used to make toys or dolls' clothes. It should be remembered that thread was very scarce in the camp and was often reused. An embroidered night-dress case made in Biberach was unpicked, re-embroidered, unpicked and re-embroidered twelve times, using the same thread, just to pass the time which weighed so heavily on the internees' hands.

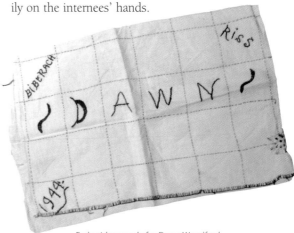

Embroidery made for Dawn Woodford by her grandmother in Biberach.

Red Cross parcel string, which was particularly prized by the women, could be woven and plaited to make a range of fashion accessories, and was assiduously collected, week by week. In order to protect the contents of the British parcels, thin strips of coloured cellophane were used as packing material. These were often retrieved from the parcels and woven into string handbags to make colourful designs. The larger pieces of cellophane from cigarette packets were cleverly folded to make belts or purses; folded cellophane created a pretty, pearlescent appearance. This 'camp fashion' was popular among many of the young women.

4

Camp life

Making personal space

The colourful cellophane strips from British Red Cross parcels were crocheted by Wurzach internee Nellie May Faulder to make decorative sleeves for small food tins, turning them into pretty trinket boxes and often decorating them with little figures or knots on the lid. Small boxes were among the most popular type of object to be made in all the camps. Whether made of wood and carved or painted (usually by men), or plaited out of parcel string (usually, but not exclusively, by women),[22] relatively large numbers of boxes survive today. When we think about how crowded the communal life was in the camps, with everyone sharing everything, we can understand the importance of having a special place to keep private objects – a little bit of space that was entirely personal.

Below and opposite - Nellie May Faulder's boxes

Nellie May Faulder

Nellie May Faulder, née Le Cocq, was born on 27th May 1908, and developed an interest in art and music from an early age. She left school aged 14 with six certificates from the Royal School of Drawing. Aged 34, when she was working as a cashier and booking clerk at the Opera House in Jersey, she was deported to Wurzach with her London-born husband Robert. While interned, she was active in recycling her old Red Cross parcels, displaying a real skill for all kinds of needlework as she crocheted and plaited the cellophane strips of packing material and parcel string to make a range of dolls, bags, brooches, belts and boxes. Although later in life Nellie May returned to her first love of drawing, it was during the years of internment that she expanded her repertoire and was able to indulge her other artistic abilities.

Left - Work basket made out of parcel string, cellophane and wool for Wurzach hospital matron Emma Ginns,

Communal living

One of the hardest aspects of camp life was the communal living. This was especially difficult for the older women, for whom taking communal showers in front of their children, a male guard, and various small boys who were the children of other women in the camp, was particularly embarrassing.[23] The incessant noise and chatter of communal, overcrowded rooms and lack of privacy was particularly trying for most, and people suffered for lack of a quiet corner to be alone. Such crowded conditions and lack of privacy are often shown in artwork as well as recorded in diaries.

A letter from Yvonne Sinclair in Biberach, written in June 1944, was published in the Channel Island Monthly Review, in which she describes the camp thus: *'Imagine long white buildings with two rings of high barbed wire, gravel, 1,000 odd people all of different classes, mix them up and there you have us. No quiet, no peace ever, nowhere to go to be alone, no privacy of any sort. When it's over we want to hide away from everyone for a while.'* [24]

Joan Coles commented in her internment diary for June 18th 1943, *'Nine months ago today since we left Jersey. I have come to the conclusion that communal living, as a system, is impossible. Perhaps it is the conditions under which we are forced to live, but there seems to be so much unrest and bad feeling amongst both men and women, that feuds are very constantly occurring. Even the children have got right out of hand, in spite of daily schooling. The feeling of fellowship in distress seems to have vanished and, sad to relate, I have become ashamed of the conduct of my fellow countrymen.'*

Left and above - Lack of privacy and noise made communal living difficult.

Communal walks

After about five months at Biberach, but earlier in Wurzach, regular walks in the local countryside were allowed for up to 125 internees at a time. The internees walked in a crocodile flanked by guards, and an Alsatian dog would run up and down the line. Places were allocated on an alphabetical basis and people took it in turns to walk. Those who didn't want to go would happily let someone else go in their place, or would sell their ticket for cigarettes. These trips outside the confines of the camp were useful safety valves for people's nerves and helped to keep internees fit and healthy. They were also a source of inspiration for artists in the camp, such as John Merry and Ethel Cheeswright, both interned in Biberach, and both of whom sketched various scenes of the countryside around the camps.

At Wurzach, the walks were very popular as they often called in at a country inn for refreshments, depending on which guard was in charge. The inn was a place where local people of the town would meet internees to exchange fresh vegetables and eggs for tinned food and cigarettes.[25] The guard in charge would turn a blind eye providing he also received some Red Cross goods.

Walks in the countryside were also very useful opportunities for collecting apples, mushrooms or strawberries, depending on the season.[26] *Wood was also collected and used for carving into objects, for painting, or for firewood, as Stanley and Doris Obott in Biberach noted in letters to the UK: 'It is very difficult to get extra walk tickets these days. Everybody is so keen to go 'wooding'. We usually gather pine cones as we find that they last longest and throw out a very good heat.'*[27]

Pencil sketch by John Merry.

5

Red Cross

Recycling Red Cross parcels

While some people recycled the wood that they collected on walks, others used only the packing cases that the parcels arrived in to make items. The cardboard parcels and the parcel string were also valued for their recycling potential. Although no recorded examples survive, some people made string bags in a fishing net style. These had a very definite use. Although some of the Red Cross food tins could be warmed up or cooked on the stoves in the rooms of the camp, others were taken to the communal kitchens where they were put into large vats of water to be heated up. Although people would write their names

The communal kitchen

on the labels of the tins, these would come off in the water, and so people soon learned to engrave their names or initials, barrack and room number on the tins themselves. The parcel string bags were used to carry tins to the kitchens. People were specially appointed, as a camp fatigue, to bring cooked tins back to the barrack rooms.

The parcel string collected by some was dyed using various foodstuffs, such as red cabbage or beetroot, to make bright colours. In the women's camp of Liebenau, the Polish internees were well known for separating the fibres of the string and plaiting individual strands to create a much finer range of string articles. A contemporary diarist recorded that *'women from Poland split the string, then, after plaiting it very finely, would sew it together to make the most beautiful articles. When, in mid-summer, the camp held an exhibition of handi-crafts in the canteen, we saw the results of their work. Out of the pieces of string they had made slippers, bags, spectacles cases, needle books, etc.'* [28] Channel Islanders in Liebenau copied the Polish women and made their own finely plaited string items. These can be recognised today as having a definite Liebenau style.

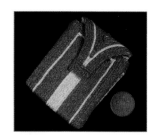

Above - A cigarette packet holder
Below - A match box cover

Most useful to many internees was the cardboard of the Red Cross parcel itself, as this could be used to make the template for soles of shoes. A piece of material from an old item of clothing was often sewn around the cardboard sole, and a plaited parcel-string base was stitched onto this, along with crocheted cellophane or a piece of material or canvas to make the upper. The canvas came from the bags of sugar sent by the Red Cross. Although the chief shoe-maker in Biberach was a Greek-American, Mr Drakos Markatos from Salonica, he soon set up a production team of ladies to mass-produce them. Letters written by many internees complain about the constant need for new shoes, both for themselves and for the children, as cardboard and string shoes were really only any good as summer sandals and soon wore out. Tales still circulate about the children of Wurzach, who used to quickly wear their out by playing hopscotch on the rough ground of the camp.

Courtesy of Carole Wheatley

High chair made from Red Cross packing case.

Internees also made very good use of the wooden packing crates in which the parcels arrived. These were made into a variety of objects, large and small. While they were useful for making items of furniture, such as deck chairs, arm-chairs for older internees, or high chairs for babies, they could also be turned into chairs for the camp theatre, or bookshelves.

Some people used the wood to make board games. Because there were never enough games to go round, despite the help of the YMCA in providing packs of cards and dominoes, Islanders made their own.

Half-made shoe showing method of manufacture

25

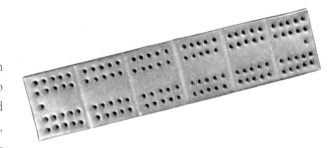

'Shove ha'penny' boards were made in Wurzach out of Red Cross packing crates. To make it smooth the hardboard was polished with noot polish from next-of-kin parcels, and real ha'pennies were collected from various people and rubbed smooth on the steps of the schloss using saliva as a lubricant.[29] A cribbage board, now on display in the Channel Islands Military Museum in Jersey

was made of wood from a Red Cross packing crate; another, in private ownership, was made from a Red Cross biscuit tin pinned onto a wooden board, with broken knitting needles used as gaming pieces. Yet a third, also privately owned, was made from a strip of leather with holes for the markers. A chess set survives from Biberach; each piece, and the board itself, was carved out of Red Cross packing-case wood; the hinges were made from a food tin. Making a chess set would have been a very time-consuming activity, which was a good thing for an internee. In order to pass the time and divert the mind away from the trials of camp life, anything that consumed time both in the making and the playing was doubly effective.

The Biberach chess set

Sports, music, theatre and carnivals: the role of the YMCA and Red Cross

The Red Cross was not the only charity that helped those deported from the Channel Islands. The YMCA supplied the camps with equipment for outdoor sports. The provision of a football enabled the inter-island Muratti to be played in Laufen. In his diary, Gerald Webb records making a trophy out of wood, which was then wrapped in silver foil.[30] Another trophy, this time for hockey, was made in Laufen from flattened and shaped Klim tins and mounted with an eagle. Tins were also recycled and used as trophies at other camps. At Biberach, Edna Dorrian remarks that, at a schoolboy Muratti, Guernsey *'got presented with a cup made of a*

margarine tin'.[31] Sports days also took place in the camps, such as that which took place on 27 April 1943 in Wurzach. Certificates were made for first, second and third places in the races, and the occasion was described as *'one of the happiest days in the camp'* since their arrival.[32]

The YMCA also provided the camps with musical equipment, writing and art materials. A cinematograph (film projector) for showing silent films, several gramophones and many records were provided at Laufen. The Red Cross would also help with procuring textbooks for studies in camp. Evening classes for the adults were very popular and schools were set up for the children in Biberach and Wurzach.

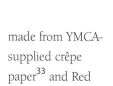

Theatres were set up in all camps and hugely well-attended plays and variety shows were held frequently, the costumes for which were made from YMCA-supplied crêpe paper[33] and Red Cross clothing. Large numbers of theatre programmes and posters survive; at Wurzach, these were painted by the talented Harold Hepburn. In Biberach, Freddy Williams and Harold Norris made the 'flats' (stage scenery) from Red Cross packing cases. A sketch of a Biberach stage set by William Sandwith noted that the set was *'constructed from Red Cross cartons, packing cases, packing wrappers and various camp oddments.'* The theatre provided much entertainment for the internees and for a short period made them forget about being behind barbed wire. As Preston John Doughty said in his Wurzach internment diary after attending a performance, *'although the Germans have got us behind barbed wire, they cannot stop us from smiling and enjoying ourselves.'* [34]

Thanks to the YMCA and their gifts of musical instruments, bands (such as the 'Swingternees' at Laufen or the 'Kreuzburg Trio' at Kreuzburg) and orchestras were formed. Some internees, such as professional musician Douglas Tanguy, had carried their instruments from home; yet others made theirs. At Wurzach, jazz drums were made out of wooden packing cases, tins and cigar boxes. Once music was established in camp, dances soon become a regular occurrence, and musical scores were sent to musicians in Biberach from Guernsey and the UK.[35]

Carnivals and fancy dress parades also took place in the camps, the most impressive of which happened at New Year 1944 in Laufen,[36] Easter Monday 1943 in Wurzach,[37] and the August Bank holiday 1943 at Biberach. The parade at Biberach was actually filmed by the camp commandant and a copy of the cine film survives to this day, as do photos of the event. These show people dressed up as a range of characters, including Uncle Sam, Justice (complete with scales and a blindfold), Boudica on her chariot, Snow White and her seven dwarfs, and Cleopatra. The carnival was described in a letter to Guernsey by Jack and Lillian Cannon thus: *'It was a very worthy show, all created from Red Cross boxes, tins, wrappings and not forgetting the beautiful dresses made out of babies' napkins... provided by the Red Cross. Cleopatra and her slaves complete with canopied conveyance were wonderfully arrayed in the above mentioned commodities and took first prize.'* [38]

August Bank Holiday 1943, Wurzach

Exhibitions of art and artefacts

The talents of various artists and artisans were recognised within the camps and it wasn't long before enough items were produced to warrant a series of handicraft exhibitions. These took place at Laufen, Biberach, Liebenau and Wurzach and diarists record that these were often timed to coincide with visits by YMCA or Red Cross representatives. Joan Coles noted in her diary that on 24 August 1944, at the third arts and crafts exhibition in Wurzach, the number of exhibits did not reach those of earlier exhibitions due to the shortage of raw materials. The previous exhibition of 23 May, which was arranged on tables made up of Canadian Red Cross boxes covered in stage scenery 'flats' from the camp theatre, displayed over 400 items, including oil and watercolour paintings, sketches, clothes, pottery, toys, baskets of paper flowers and model planes. In his internment diary, Mike Shepherd described an exhibition of arts and crafts held at Wurzach, saying that *'some of the exhibits were marvellous and it seemed unbelievable that they had been made in the camp. There were slippers made from string, belts made from coloured paper, drawings and paintings. Most of the materials were obtained from the Red Cross parcels, whilst the paper for the drawings came from Switzerland'.*

In Biberach, the frequency of the 'occupational therapy' exhibitions is neatly captured in the colourful and professional exhibition posters made by Eric Sirett, a talented commercial artist, six of which still survive, illustrated with images of handicrafts made in the camps. Ron Harris described one of these exhibitions in a letter home. *'Among the exhibits was the hand-produced baptismal certificate of a child born here last August. The other exhibits included toys, drawings, paintings, needlework, stringwork and metalwork. Except for the drawing materials and needlework, everything is improvised from the packing and string of parcels.'* [39]

31

Posters designs by
Eric Sirett

Representatives from the Red Cross and YMCA would visit the camps irregularly and internees would make requests for certain items through their room and barrack block leaders. Initially, it seems that people wrote to these organisations direct, but this was stopped in November 1943 owing to a desire on the part of the Red Cross to avoid duplication and wastage, and because of the difficulty in obtaining supplies. After this date, they requested that items be used for the benefit of the camp as a whole rather than just for individuals.

Diary entries, memoirs and items in museums attest to the presence of additional items not on the original German deportation order, which some internees fitted in their suitcases and trunks and brought with them to the camps. These items helped some to make their artwork. Eric Sirett recorded that Ruth, his wife, packed her *'scissors, hair clippers, tail combs and even small curling tongs, while I managed to stow away a small box of water colours, some bottles of poster colours, brushes, pencils and two sketch pads. Two men actually carried small sewing machines that were worth their weight in gold to the internees, one man using his to produce lots of battle dress type suits out of the grey German blankets.'*

Eric Sirett

Eric John Lewis Sirett was born in Farnborough on the 3rd October, 1920. He studied art at Chiswick Polytechnic and, on completion of his studies, came to Guernsey, where his family had holidayed in the 1920s, and was employed at the Star newspaper as a compositor. He met and married Ruth Gallienne, a local hairdresser, and they ended up having an extended honeymoon abroad in Biberach camp.

Eric's artistic abilities, coupled with the paints, brushes and paper he took with him to camp, which the YMCA also supplemented, allowed his talents to shine. He was called upon to design posters to advertise camp events, such as the exhibitions of arts and crafts. He sketched portraits and he designed beautiful greetings cards for Ruth, complete with clever poems about camp life. His personal archive comprises notes, poems, songs, pictures and photographs taken while in camp, the latter of which was made possible by bartering 100 cigarettes with a German guard in exchange for a camera and film.

6

Childood in the camps

Keeping children entertained became an important part of daily life for mothers in the family camps. The crying and noise of the children could grate on the nerves of people who shared their crowded rooms, but generally it was more normal for everyone to pitch in and help, or for several women with small children to share a room together. The children slept with their mothers in the women's rooms or barracks and, in line with societal norms of the time, it was the women's job to look after the children.

The children of the camp should not be perceived as having been 'just a nuisance' to everyone; they had their own rich social lives and adventures, many of which can be told by those internees alive today, who were children or teenagers in camps. It is a sad fact that very few or almost none of the adults in the camp (i.e. those with families and responsibilities) are alive today, and so it is mostly the testimony of the younger deportees that are still available to be recorded. For the most part, this age group was spared the fears and worries of their parents and, for some, the experience of internment was, paradoxically, a time of freedom for them: freedom for most teenagers from school or work; freedom from fatigues for the under 16s (although some chose to go out of the camp and run errands with a German attendant, because of the

perks involved in being able to acquire the odd extra piece of food or fuel), and freedom to roam beyond the sight of their parents and play with their friends for most of the day. We must also remember that some young people were among those who died during internment or who lost family members, so some also had to bear heavy burdens of grief at a young age, which affect them still to this day.

Several toys made in the camps still survive. Among these are included rag dolls made by women in Biberach.

Rag doll made in Biberach from scraps of material for Beryl Kellow

One woman interned in Wurzach, Mrs Florence Fish, made nearly 100 'Heidi' dolls from scraps of material provided by fellow internees. The hair, hat and basket were made from parcel string and the doll's socks were made from bandages. On donating it to the British Red Cross archives, she wrote that *'the reason I began making dolls was that we had 200 children with us, mostly little girls. They, at that time, had nothing to play with so I started collecting scraps of material and that is how it all began … the only pleasant thing that stays in my memory are the faces of the little girls when they had their dollies, even though they were only rag ones.'* [40] Painted images of these dolls also survive, no doubt inspired by the Alps, which were sometimes visible from the camp or seen during walks.

British Red Cross Museum and Archives

One of the small dolls made by Nellie May Faulder in Wurzach. The doll has a wooden body, a painted face and woollen hair. Her dress is made from crocheted strips of coloured cellophane.

The toys made for children by men tended to be carved from wood; an example can be seen in a 'pecking hens' toy made in Biberach. An exception to this rule were the leather farmyard

animals made by Guernseyman Fred Martel, who had been the cobbler in Beghin's shoe shop in St Peter Port before he was deported. His skill in working with leather led to him being sent from Biberach to Liebenau in February 1944 with his family in order to mend shoes at the camp; at the time, he was the only man there and was nicknamed 'the King of Liebenau'. Mr Martel used his leather off-cuts to make toy animals for his small son, Michael.

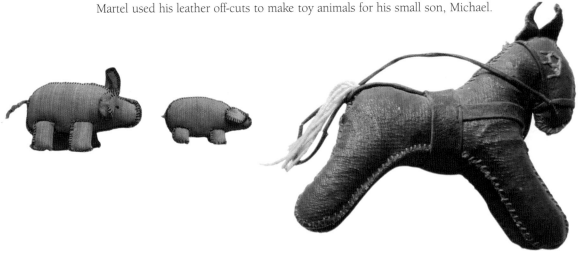

Several internment diaries record how people would get together to make toys for the children at Christmas. Joan Coles records that, at Wurzach in 1942, *'fragments from Red Cross parcels'* and *'bits of material'* were *'made into quaint animals and numerous little wooden toys, all made in the camp.'* At Biberach, the men set up a production line in December 1943, making wooden cots for the girls and wooden cranes for the boys. Ron Harris wrote from Biberach that *'on the 23rd December there was a fine party for the children … each child had a toy made by men in the camp. I've never seen such wonderful things turned out of bits of firewood: planes, dolls' cots, wheel-barrows, cranes, etc, and when you think that there are over a hundred children here you can guess what it was like'.*[41] By the third Christmas in captivity, people were becoming more inventive and skilled in the items they were able to make out of recycled materials for the children. In Biberach, Rose Dawe's father made her a toy cooking stove, complete with pots, pans and various kitchen utensils, from Red Cross tins.

Toy production line in Biberach

Two further sources of information about childhood in the camps come from photographs and artwork. A very small number of post-liberation photos survive from Biberach, one of which shows a child's toy pram made from flattened tins, the wheels made from tin lids. A watercolour from Wurzach depicts

Carole Wheatley with doll's pram made from Red Cross tins.

Courtesy of Carole Wheatley

children playing in the sandpit and on a see-saw at the front of the schloss. Another painting shows a room complete with children's toys strewn around the floor and beds. A doll's bed and pushchair are clearly visible on the floor. The beauty of this painting is that it shows us toys which no longer survive, and which were made from recycled Red Cross parcels.

Christmas time behind barbed wire

Christmas was a special time in the camps. Parties and meals were arranged for the children and the camps were imaginatively decorated with items from Red Cross parcels. Joan Coles described how the decorations of the first Christmas in Wurzach were made from recycled materials. *'Most Red Cross parcels contained shredded cellophane and this became quite a useful commodity for craft work and to trim the Christmas trees which were brought into the camp. All rooms were gaily decorated with crêpe paper, chains, bright festoons, mostly obtained from Red Cross parcels, [although] some had been passed in by the German guards. Christmas trees were brought in from the village and placed in the larger rooms, where they were later trimmed with small gifts of chocolate, cigarettes and handmade articles.'*

At Christmas time in Laufen in 1942, Gerald Webb wrote in his diary that while he was out of the camp on fatigues, he came across a small Christmas tree. *'I took it into our room, decorated it with Christmas candles, silver paper and cigarette boxes.'* However at the same time the following year, he wrote that *'our room was the poorest of the lot, except for a couple of Christmas trees and the good old Union Jack. There isn't much else - we haven't any heart.'* It sounded like the family camps were a far more cheerful place to be at Christmas. However, not everyone was cheerful there, as shown by a humorous Christmas card designed by Eric Sirett, which compared Biberach to Hell.

using it to confuse radar was called 'Operation Window').

Other Christmas decorations known at Biberach were made from Player's Navy Cut

The silver paper that Gerald Webb referred to on the previous page, that was used to decorate Christmas trees, was probably the strips of aluminium foil that fell in several of the camp grounds. These were dropped by Allied and German planes to block or confuse radar signals, but also caused problems with radio reception. The German version of this was called 'Düppel', and the British, 'chaff' or 'window' (so called because the technique of

cigarette packets, which were recycled into little lanterns and hung on the tree.[42] As all adult internees over 16 were given a weekly ration of cigarettes, there were plenty of empty boxes around. The few non-smokers were able to exchange their cigarettes with smokers for Red Cross food, or were able to 'pay' other internees to perform their fatigues for them.

7

Art and artists in the camps

The first Christmas away from the Channel Islands was the catalyst for the beginnings of a camp hobby which grew with time and remained extremely popular throughout the period of internment: the fashion for making greetings cards. In November 1943, for example, a month before Christmas, Gerald Webb recorded in his diary *'the craze about camp at present is the drawing of Christmas cards to send away. Everyone is busy.'*

The work of certain talented artists in camp crops up in many personal collections in the Channel Islands today. Among others, we might include William Henry Sandwith, a commercial artist who was deported to Biberach. His cards often depict the view beyond the barbed wire as seen from the camp.

Greetings cards by Sandwith

41

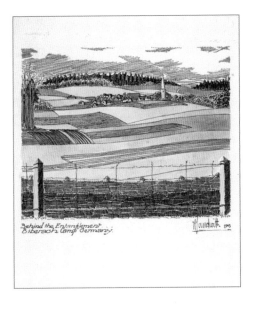

Painting by John Merry

John Merry was another very talented artist in Biberach, and he favoured views of barrack rooms and the town itself. At Wurzach, the most ubiquitous maker of cards and posters was Harold Hepburn, who favoured cards depicting views of the Schloss, often drawn with his trademark images of RAF Spitfires and German helmets and swastikas in opposite corners of the cards. Leslie Greenwood was another popular Wurzach artist. He painted images from everyday life in the camps, writing the word 'Wurzach' above his artwork in gothic German script. Thomas Webber, formerly a builder's labourer, discovered in Wurzach that he could draw. His beautiful greetings cards often depict flowers or images of Father Time and the blindfolded figure of Justice, implying that the internees would, in time, have justice and be released. Artists who found fame inside Laufen included Henry Barnett, who designed the camp Christmas cards in 1943 and 1944, and who also gave art classes in camp.

Because of the extreme shortage of paper during the early days and towards the end of internment, the craze for card making peaked and troughed at different times. In fact, paper was so scarce at certain times in Laufen that internees would even resort to using treasured letters from friends and relatives as toilet paper.[43] A keen correspondent from Biberach, Ron Harris, also recorded on 6 April 1943 that *'paper in any form is quite unobtainable, and but for my foresight in bringing a personal stock our position would have been pretty desperate. The majority here have suffered the most distressing difficulty and privation in this respect.'* [44]

Painting and sketching buildings outside the camp were very popular. It was common practice, especially among camp artists, to exchange their ration of cigarettes with the guards for postcards of the local town. These were used as the main inspiration in art classes for the many watercolours of local scenes that were produced. Because of this, it is not uncommon to see a single image reproduced exactly by a number of different artists in camp.

Occupied Behind Barbed Wire

Other views and themes were particularly popular among the professional and amateur artists, such as images of their camps and camp grounds (complete with watchtowers) and views through the barbed wire. Views of

The artists were luckier than most in having an outlet for their frustrations as shown in a watercolour of an artist taking out his pent-up anger on his canvas.

Imperial War Museum

rooms are plentiful, and represented an internee's 'home' within the camp. Because of the importance of the room for each internee, or, more specifically, the space around their bed, this view was represented on a number of items, including greetings cards, watercolours, an engraved mug, a tapestry and even a wooden model.

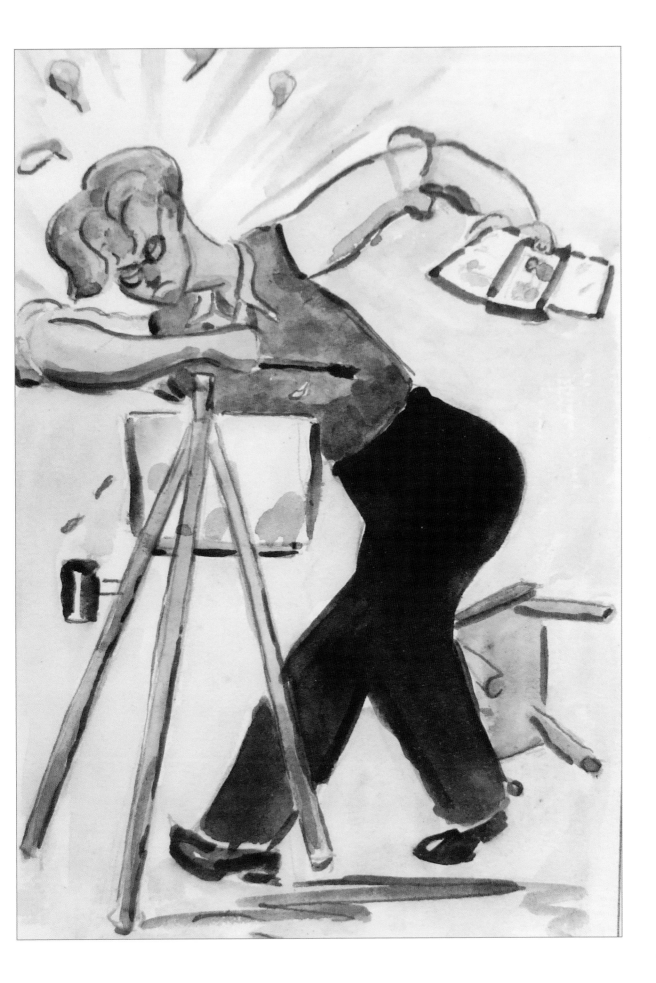

We shouldn't imagine that art in the camps was restricted to a small number of talented people. Judging from private and public collections in the Channel Islands, it seems that most people tried their hand at painting or drawing at one time or another. As one former internee at Wurzach remarked, *'all sorts of people developed hobbies that they probably had an interest in but never worked at in their life in Jersey. I was amazed at the number of budding artists we had … we tried to do anything that would take our minds off the war.'* [45]

Because greetings cards were the most ubiquitous item made in the camps, most former internees have a small collection of those given to them and their parents. The usual range of special occasions was commemorated in this way by exchange between friends and family: Easter, birthdays, anniversaries, Christmas and New Year all rolled around slowly but inevitably for each year in captivity. Each year, the hope was recorded that this year would be the last in captivity and next year would be celebrated back in the Channel Islands.

Harold Hepburn

Harold Hepburn was born on 4th August 1907, and lived in St Saviour in Jersey. He worked as a commercial sign painter and, until he was deported to Wurzach with his wife Dorothy and daughter, Mary Rose, didn't realise his full potential as an artist. As a former internee who knew Hepburn in the camp put it, 'when he had time to sit down, he found he could draw pictures too.' When going out for walks, Hepburn would see churches and the beautiful old buildings of Wurzach, and keep the images in his mind. When back in the Schloss, he'd sit with the postcard and paint pictures. His trademark was a swastika pennant on one side and three Spitfires on the other, so if he was challenged, he couldn't be accused of disseminating British propaganda.[46]

Hepburn frequently depicted comic scenes of camp life and various images that were personal to the receiver of the cards, although his most common choice of image was the Schloss itself, drawn from various angles. Because of his talents as a sign-writer, Hepburn was much in demand for producing sports certificates and camp posters, whether for theatres, boxing matches, or sports events.

No place like home

These poignant Christmas wishes were often accompanied by unusual or unexpected images. For example, a number of Christmas cards depicted a traditional English village or a cottage complete with thatched roofs, leaded windows and roses around the front door. Very occasionally, this scene was replaced with a traditional Channel Island farmhouse, but more often it was a definitely English scene; not surprising when we remember that most internees were deported because they were English-born. The best example of such a card was painted at Christmas in Laufen, and depicts a traditional English country village in the middle of summer, with hollyhocks in full bloom. This type of card was obviously a generic scene of 'home', and represented the ultimate heart's desire for all internees; thus, it made a meaningful present when given to other internees, especially when we consider the grave shortages of paper in the camps at various times.

Images of a traditional English home were popular in a number of different media. While examples exist in sketches and watercolours, it is also something that crops up on painted boxes, badges and embroidered postcards. Joan Coles was skilled in embroidery and needlework, and regularly produced items for the Wurzach camp exhibitions of arts and crafts. At least three embroidered miniature pictures by Coles, a postcard and two little brooches, show idyllic English country cottages with flowers around the doorway.

Images of the Channel Islands are also relatively numerous, and can be interpreted in the same way, i.e. as images of home. What is special about these images is that, in contrast to the pictures of generic English villages and cottages drawn from the imagination, they depict specific landmarks and were drawn from memory. Examples of this include two badges made out of knots of wood, which depict Corbière lighthouse and Janvrin's

tomb in Jersey. Greetings cards and watercolours were also popular media for depicting landmarks. A very detailed pen and ink sketch of Castle Cornet in Guernsey was drawn on a 1944 Biberach wedding anniver-

sary card, but the most impressive artwork in this category was a painting by Sark artist Ethel Cheeswright. This was made as a thank you gift for Dr Fleischer in Biberach, who had helped internees in the camp, and is now in the possession of his widow. It is among Cheeswright's most beautiful paintings and depicts a view of the cliffs of Sark covered in spring flowers. It is a view that she often painted during her lifetime but the example made in the camp is more glorious, obviously seen at the height of its beauty in her mind's eye. In the letters to the editor section of the September 1943 issue of the *Channel Island Monthly Review*, her views of the Channel Islands painted in camp were reported to have *'moistened the eyes of the ladies a little'.*

Another way in which islanders were able to metaphorically bring 'home' into the camps, was to set about transforming a very small part of the grey and drab camp grounds inside the barbed wire into a traditional English (or Channel Island) country garden. Two watercolours painted by internees show how this was attempted at Biberach. The first, by Sidney Skillett, shows a garden in full bloom, sunflowers growing side by side with lettuces and cauliflowers, with the barracks in the background. Quite how this was possible is revealed by Garfield Garland, who listed his thanks to various organisations who were able to help the internees during their time in the camp, including the British Seedsmen and the Royal Horticultural Society, who sent seeds. Garland reports that the Camp Gardening Department were able to convert several parts of the camp's grounds into kitchen gardens, and the camp gardener and some inmates had also planted flower beds in front of some of their barracks, which added *considerable cheer to the camp*.

One of Ethel Cheeswright's paintings shows a delightful view of the camp with neat grass and the flowerbeds in full bloom. The greenery seems to meld with the landscape beyond the barbed wire, somehow making the watchtower and wire lose their sting.

Such colour paintings give a gentler view of the camp when compared to drab black and white photographs of Biberach. Some of these photos of internees toiling in the camp garden, or the garden freshly dug, waiting for the seeds to be sewn, still survive.

Channel Islanders' gardens, and especially their flowers, are famed for their beauty just as much as traditional English country gardens. Many internees painted or made flowers from a variety of raw materials during their hours of incarceration, bringing colour and cheer to the camp.

Included among these home-made blooms were some made in Liebenau, by Guernseywoman Norah Martel, out of vegetable-dyed Red Cross parcel string and cellophane; a sampler made in Biberach by internee Jill Oliver when she was a child; and a wooden tray painted with colourful and exotic flowers, a 35th birthday present in Biberach *'from Will to Trixie'*; and Byll Balcombe's engraved mugs feature flowers, filling the space between the main images, a motif repeated on every piece of his work. A sampler made in Biberach by internee Patricia Bell in 1943 is decorated with birds, trees, flowers and, at the bottom, riders in pink jackets with their hounds, chasing a stag. The majority of all embroidered and crocheted women's bags made in the camps are also decorated with these symbols of nature.

Flower badges made from string

Some of the imagery engraved, embroidered or crocheted on artefacts shows generic images of freedom, features of landscapes such as birds, flowers, butterflies, and animals; the nature and wildlife that so characterise the beautiful islands and the English countryside from which the internees came.

8

Identity, Resistance and V-signs in the camps

Overt resistance in the civilian internment camps did not happen for fear of reprisals against family members or the arrival of the Gestapo in the camp. Because of this, the resistance was similar in some respects to that which had been common in the Islands before their deportation. This included the manufacture of radios (e.g. the 'Forbidden whisper' made in Laufen, as recorded by Frank Stroobant,[47] or the crystal set made in Kreuzburg[48]) and illicit listening to the BBC, which also took place at other camps.[49]

The V-sign campaign, so popular in the Islands, continued in the camps through the use of the V-for-victory sign, which was incorporated as a thinly veiled symbol in artwork and handicrafts made by internees. In the summer of 1941, Islanders had listened to the BBC's English-speaking European service, which had broadcast an appeal to the occupied peoples of Europe to paint V-signs on doors and walls and gates to make the Germans feel that they were surrounded by an invisible army of anti-German resistance fighters. The V-sign campaign had enjoyed a brief period of popularity that summer, but the Germans had acted swiftly to quash it. In reality, all they had done was to push it underground. One example of this was the manufacture of V-sign badges by two Guernseymen, several examples of which were worn in Biberach.[50]

Talented Biberach artist, Eric Sirett, produced a pencil sketch of 'Monty' Manning, former Scout-master and one of the adults in charge of the young boys' barracks in the camp. Manning is clearly shown sporting a beard and a moustache cut into a V-shape; the caption makes it clear that this was deliberate. To German guards, Manning was probably seen as an eccentric Englishman, but to other

internees, Manning was a walking V-sign, and his appearance must have provoked much laughter and good cheer in camp. A similar example is seen on a woman's rope-soled

shoe made in Wurzach, which has a V-sign made from plaited Red Cross parcel string on

its sole. This would have left the most marvellous footprints around camp, especially when wet. The evidence of this resistance would soon dry and disappear, preferably before the guards had seen it.

Other Vs were not intended to be as humorous; they existed simply to boost morale in camp and provide an invisible bond of solidarity with friends and family left behind in the Islands through the use of symbols that were probably meaningless to the guards (who in any case had been 'trained' or bribed by internees to turn a blind eye and not inter-

fere too much in affairs in the camp), but not to other internees. Examples of these are numerous and include a mug engraved with a large V-sign by internee Byll Balcombe, enabling him to drink a toast to victory . On the bottom of Balcombe's many engraved mugs is an image of the profile of Mount Everest above a small V-sign. When turned sideways, this turns into the profile of a man's face (probably that of Balcombe himself) and the V-sign turns into the eye.

Other examples of Vs incorporated into the items made in camp include a V-shaped scissors case, decorated with Vs, and made in Liebenau.[51] Morale was also boosted by making the link between the V-sign and patriotism, as seen in an embroidered tablecloth made in Wurzach, dedicated in the centre to George V by the use of his monogram and an image of a crown on a cushion. Coloured Vs decorate the edges of the cloth. While this could have been explained away, if challenged by a guard, as a patriotic dedication to the king, George VI was actually the reigning monarch at this time and had been on the throne since 1936.

Vs were also used to create camaraderie between fellow internees. As Gerald Webb reported in his internment diary on New Year's Eve 1942, a group of Channel Islander internees in Laufen made a gift for the Greek contingent in their camp: a *'decorated box containing the Greek and British national colours in silk and a large V-sign with the year 1943 set in between'*.[52] Camaraderie and friendships were also cemented and celebrated by the exchange of greetings cards on special occasions. Several depict V-signs, some-

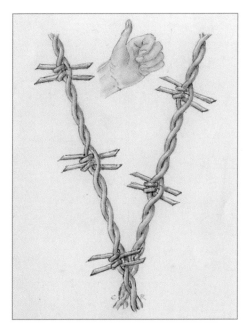

times in patriotic colours. V-signs were also employed on other special occasions, such as Christmas. A solitary part of a Christmas dec-

oration exists in a private collection in the form of a V-sign made of roundels of sailors' faces, cut from boxes of Player's Navy Cut cigarettes, slotted together, and hung on the wall at a children's Christmas party.

Jersey War Tunnels

We know from paintings and rare photos of barrack rooms that room decorations such as painted pictures and Union Jacks existed all year round. As a Biberach camp pencil sketch by John Merry of room 15 in barrack 6 testifies, internees also placed V-signs above the doorways of their rooms; this same view is also rendered as an embroidery by the same artist, and is in the German Occupation Museum in Guernsey.

This is probably because Colman's mustard had a Union Jack on the label; however, it seems that some Wurzach internees got hold of these, because the flags were cut out, pasted on to wood or cardboard, and turned into badges. One former Biberach internee also recalls wearing a paper Colman's mustard Union Jack.[54] Union Jack badges were also

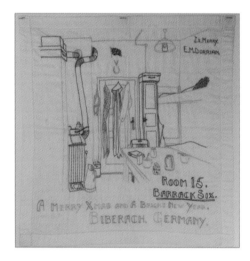

Other forms of resistance in camp involved the defiant display of British identity by hanging Union Jacks in rooms or wearing Union Jack badges. A number of these still exist, made from a variety of materials such as wool, beads, coloured thread, wood and buttons. Interestingly, in his Wurzach memoirs, Mike Shepherd comments that mustard was prohibited from Red Cross parcels.[53]

worn by the Channel Island football team at Laufen during their matches with the Americans in camp. These badges acquired a second use after the camp was liberated, when internees used to walk into the local town wearing their badges to prove their identity so that the liberating French or American armies would not mistake them for German civilians.

55

The Laufen CI football team wearing their Union Jacks.

9

Liberation

Liberation of the camps took place at different times. For those in Biberach, Wurzach and Liebenau, for example, it was 23, 28 and 29 April respectively, and all were liberated by Free French troops. Those in Laufen were liberated on 4 May by the Americans. Aside from Union Jack badges, the number of items made to commemorate this long-awaited and joyous occasion were few and far between. Now that the internees were free, they didn't want to spend their time indoors, making items, when they were able to explore the local towns and landscape at will (although a curfew was placed on them for their own safety).

As in the early days of internment, a craze for collecting autographs emerged, judging from the dates in autograph books owned by former internees. However, instead of signatures, most people would paint little signed watercolours, some of which also commemorated their liberation.

Two pieces of work made at this time stand out above the others. The first is a greetings card made by Harold Hepburn. In a departure from his usual theme of Schloss Wurzach filling the frame, flanked by images of British planes and swastikas, this time the image is reversed and the swastika has vanished. Visually dominating the card is a

Dakota aeroplane, flying the internees back home. The Schloss and the town of Wurzach are reduced to tiny buildings in the background, and the plane's smoke trail reads *'Goodbye Wurzach!'*

To commemorate Biberach's liberation, Byll Balcombe made his finest piece of work. Picking up one of the discarded shell cases left behind by fleeing German soldiers, he carefully engraved it with an image of the outline of the island of Guernsey, draped with freesias. Above this is inscribed a prayer in Guernesiaise, the Guernsey patois: *'L'Eternal nous protège! I'nous ordoune, amis, d'aimair la*

bénite ile ou sa grâce nous a mis!' ('The Eternal protect us! He orders us, friends, to love the blessed isle where his grace settled us!') On the other side, Balcombe engraved an image of the 'Weberberg', an area of the town often drawn by internees during their confinement. With an image of a rising sun, the caption commemorates the barbed-wire-entwined names of the internees for whom it was made, and the date of liberation of the camp by the French in April 1945.

Clock wise from top right - A crowd of Channel Islanders gather to greet their liberators.

Suitcases ready - waiting to go home.

The arrival of Allied troops.

Byll Balcombe's engraved shell case. Multiple views.

Graham Jackson Photography

Bibliography

Carr, G. (2008). 'The trench art of Byll Balcombe of Biberach', *Channel Islands Occupation Review* 36, 131-145.

Coles, J. (1985). *Three Years Behind Barbed Wire*. Jersey: La Haule Books Ltd.

Cruikshank, C. (1990) [1975]. *The German Occupation of the Channel Islands*. Sutton Publishing Ltd (OUP).

Dorrian, E. Internment diary, unpublished. Guernsey Archives ref. AQ 299/22 (1-16)

Doughty, P.J. *I was there: our trip on the continent*. Unpublished manuscript. Jersey Archive ref. L/C/46/A/2.

Garland, G. (1944). *A report to the British Red Cross on conditions at Biberach September 1944*. Unpublished manuscript, Priaulx Library ref. LF940.53 LEN.

Garland, G. (1945). *A brief history of the Guernsey Deportees to Dorsten and Biberach, Germany. September 1942-June 1945*. Unpublished manuscript, Priaulx Library ref. LF940.53 LEN.

Green, Leslie. *My War Years*. Unpublished manuscript. Société Jersiaise library ref. OCC.942.GRE.

Harris, R.E. (1979). *Islanders Deported*. Part I. Ilford: CISS Publishing.

Red Cross (1942). *Prisoner of War: The first authentic account of the lives of British prisoners of war in enemy hands*. Published by Horace Marshall and Sons Ltd, London.

Saunders, N. (2001). *Trench Art: a brief history and guide, 1914-1939*. Barnsley: Leo Cooper.

Saunders, N. (2003). *Trench Art: materialities and memories of war*. Oxford and New York: Berg.

Shepherd, M. *Behind Wire*. Unpublished manuscript. Jersey Heritage Trust ref. L/D/25/A/70.

Sinel, L. (1945). *The German Occupation of Jersey 1940-1945*. Jersey: Jersey Evening Post.

Stroobant, F. (1997) [1967]. *One Man's War*. Guernsey: Burbridge Ltd.

Tough, K. (1995). 'Deportation from Guernsey 1942 – two personal accounts and a German assessment.', *Channel Islands Occupation Review* 20, 63-76.

Webb, G. Internment diary. Unpublished manuscript. Guernsey Island Archives, ref. AQ 78/10.

Acknowledgements

The author would like to thank the following groups of people for their help, advice and contribution of material for this book.

Museum owners, curators and archivists: Chris Addy (Jersey War Tunnels), Paul and Peter Balshaw (La Valette Military Museum, Guernsey), Amanda Bennett and Gillian Lenfestey (Priaulx Library, Guernsey), Matt Harvey (Guernsey Museums & Galleries), Richard Heaume (German Occupation Museum), Damien Horn (Channel Islands Military Museum), Alan Jeffreys (Imperial War Museum), Neil Mahrer, Val Nelson, Stuart Nicolle and Linda Romeril (Jersey Heritage), Darryl Ogier (Island Archives, Guernsey), and Jen Young (British Red Cross Museum and Archive).

Members of the Guernsey Deportee Association, especially Tom Remfrey, and all former internees in Biberach, Liebenau and Laufen, including Gwen Ashton, Gwen Barnett, Doris Bougourd, Doreen Brouard, Bob Chilcott, Chris Day, Angela Eker, Irene Harvey, Nellie Le Feuvre, Stephen Matthews, Mike Martel, George and Brenda Norman, Jill Oliver, Pat O'Brien, Yvonne Osborn, Janet de Santos, Irene Shorrock, Colin Skillet, David Skillett, Ron Snell, Audrey and Reginald Thomason, Jean Wakeham, John Way, Carole Wheatley, Norma Wilson and Bill Wilton.

All former members of the Ex-Internee Association in Jersey and former internees in Wurzach, Laufen and Kreuzburg, particularly Michael and Josephine Ginns and Angela Trigg, but also: Gwen Bisson, John Burges, Mary Cornish, Sylvia Diamond, Ursula Dingle, Victor Graham, John Green, Irene Grubb, Patricia Holt, Sheila Legg, Maurice and Henry Matthews, Maisie Plain, Kathleen Richardson, Douglas Tanguy, Pamela Tanguy, Maurien Venables and William Waghorn.

Other Islanders, some of whom are relatives of former internees, including Christine Bailey, Jon Bartlett, Peter Boon, Harriet Carré, John Cadot, Peter and Rose Druckes, Jim Duffield, John Goodwin, Simon Hamon, Sally Hutchins, Anne Long, John Maine, Jan McKayne, Robin Millard, Mark Norman, Frances Quin, Peter Sirett, Rebekah Skipper, Paul Wakeham and Neil Walker.

Biberach historian Reinhold Adler, Wurzach historian Gisela Rothenhausler, members of the Biberach Friends of Guernsey, and Heidi and Werner Drews who looked after me while I was in Biberach.

End notes

1 P.J. Doughty, I was there: our trip on the continent, p.2. Jersey Archive ref. L/C/46/A/2.

2 Interview with Michael Ginns, Jersey War Tunnels ref. 2007/1022.

3 Sinel, L. 1945. The German Occupation of Jersey 1940-1945: a complete diary. Jersey Evening Post: Jersey.

4 Note by Florence Fish accompanying archive donation, British Red Cross Museum and Archive accession number 0054(2).

5 Edna Dorrian's diary entry for 29/4/43, 1/5/43 and 4/5/43.

6 Edna Dorrian's diary entry for 5/1/43 and 29/12/43.

7 Joan Coles, entry for 13/12/42. Three Years Behind Barbed Wire: the diary of a British Internee in 'Schloss Wurzach', Germany, 1942-1945: La Haule Books, Jersey.

8 Tough, K. 1995, 70.

9 Leslie Green, My War Years. p. 21. Société Jersiaise library ref. occ.942.gre.

10 From Eric Sirett's archive, courtesy of Peter Sirett.

11 Letter from Jack and Lillian Cannon in Biberach to Clarice and Larry Langerd in Guernsey, 26/1/43. Courtesy of Robin Millard.

12 Interview with Michael Ginns, Jersey War Tunnels ref. 2007/1022.

13 Letter from Jack and Lillian Cannon in Biberach to Larry Langerd in Guernsey, 18/4/43. Courtesy of Robin Millard.

14 Letter written by Jack and Lillian Cannon in Biberach to Larry Langerd in Guernsey, 8/3/43. Courtesy of Robin Millard.

15 Letter written by Jack and Lillian Cannon in Biberach to Larry Langerd in Guernsey, 4/8/43. Courtesy of Robin Millard.

16 Mike Shepherd, Behind Wire. Jersey Archive L/D/25/A/70.

17 Interview with Patricia Holt, Jersey, 20/8/08.

18 Channel Island Monthly Review, September 1944, vol. 7(3), 55.

19 P.J. Doughty I was there: our trip on the continent. p.14. Jersey Archive ref. L/C/46/A/2.

20 Interview with Yvonne Osborn, 21/8/2008.

21 Interview with Michael Ginns, 18/8/2008.

22 Mr Bill Grimshaw used to make work baskets out of parcel string. My thanks to Mrs Sheila Legg for showing me her father's work.

23 Tough, K. 1995, 69.

24 Channel Island Monthly Review October 1944, vol. 7(4), 71.

25 Interview with Michael Ginns on 11/09/06, Jersey War Tunnels archive.

26 Extract from diary of Norah Martel, 1944.

27 Letter from Stanley and Doris Obott in Biberach to UK, 28/10/44. Prisoner of War correspondence, Interlude at Biberach 1942-1945, courtesy of the CIOS, Jersey.

28 Feuerheerd, A.S. 'You had to be lucky: a record of my war reminiscences 1939-1945.' British Red Cross Museum and Archive ref. 106/1.

29 Interview with Michael Ginns, Jersey, 18/8/08.

30 Gerald Webb, unpublished internment diary, 19/4/1945. Guernsey Island Archive, ref. AQ 78/10

31 Edna Dorrian's unpublished internment diary, 29/4/1943. Guernsey Island Archives ref. AQ 299/22(1-16).

32 Joan Coles, 1985. Entry for 27/4/1943. Three Years Behind Bars. Jersey: La Haule Books.

33 Joan Coles, 1985. Entry for 6/9/1943. Three Years Behind Bars. Jersey: La Haule Books.

34 P.J. Doughty, entry for 26/9/1943. I was there: our trip on the continent (unpublished manuscript). Jersey Archive ref. L/C/46/A/2.

35 Interview with Yvonne Osborn, 21/8/08.

36 Gerald Webb, entry for 4/1/1944. Unpublished diary. Island Archive, Guernsey, ref. AQ 78/10.

37 Joan Coles, 1985. Entry for 26/4/43. Three Years Behind Bars. Jersey: La Haule Books.

38 Letter by Jack and Lillian Cannon to Larry Langerd in Guernsey, 4/9/43. Courtesy of Robin Millard.

39 Letter from Ron Harris to UK, 12/2/1944. British Red Cross Museum and Archive ref. 2378.

40 Donation letter accompanying Heidi doll, made by Mrs Florence Fish in Wurzach, British Red Cross Museum and Archive accession number 0054(1).

41 Letter from Ron and Eileen Harris in Biberach, 28/12/1943. British Red Cross Museum and Archive ref. 2378.

42 Interview with Yvonne Osborn, 18/3/2008.

43 Leslie Green, My War Years, p. 34. Société Jersiaise library ref. occ.942.gre.

44 Correspondence between Ron and Eileen Harris in Biberach and their families, 6/4/43, British Red Cross Museum and Archive ref. 2378.

45 John Green interviewed at Jersey War Tunnels, ref. 2007/973.

46 Interview with Michael Ginns on 11/9/06, Jersey War Tunnels archive.

47 Stroobant, F. 1967.

48 Interview with Douglas Tanguy, Jersey, 10/4/2008.

49 Letter from Stanley and Doris Obott in Biberach to UK, 21/5/05. Prisoner of War correspondence, Interlude at Biberach 1942-1945, courtesy of the CIOS, Jersey.

50 Examples exist in the archives of Candie Gardens Museum and Art Gallery; thanks also to Mark Norman and Peter Sirett in Guernsey for showing me their parents' V-sign badges that were taken to Biberach.

51 British Red Cross Museum and Archive ref. 0551/18.

52 Island Archives, Guernsey, ref. AQ 78/10.

53 Mike Shepherd, Behind Wire. Unpublished manuscript, p. 115. Jersey Archive ref. L/D/25/A/70.

54 Interview with Audrey Thomason, February 2007.

Brief chronology of the Deportations

1939

1 September German forces invade Poland.

3 September Britain declares war against Germany.

1940

1 July German forces occupy the Channel Islands.

1942

15 September Official notice ordering the deportation of British subjects published in the *Evening Post* (Jersey).

16 September Official notice ordering the deportation of British subjects published in the *Evening Press* (Guernsey).

16 September First group of deportees leave Jersey.

18 September Second group of deportees leave Jersey.

26 September First group of deportees leave Guernsey and Sark.

27 September Second group of deportees leave Guernsey.

29 September Third group of deportees leave Jersey.

3rd October British commandos raid Sark - Operation Basalt.

1943

12 February Third group of deportees leave Guernsey.

13 February Fourth group of deportees leave Jersey

25 February Fourth and final group of deportees leave Guernsey (mainly from Sark).

25 February Fifth and final group of deportees leave Jersey.

1945

23 April Biberach liberated by Free French troops.

28 April Wurzach liberated by Free French troops.

29 April Libenau liberated by Free French troops.

30 April Hitler commits suicide.

4 May Laufen liberated by American troops.

8 May VE Day – Germany surrenders.

9 May Jersey and Guernsey liberated.

10 May Sark liberated.

June Channel Island deportees repatriated to the UK.

Byll Balcombe's engraved shell case.
(Graham Jackson Photography)

First published Jersey 2009

By the Jersey Heritage Trust
Jersey Museum, The Weighbridge, St Helier,
Jersey, JE2 3NG

ISBN 978-0-9552508-4-2

Text © Dr Gillian Carr
Illustrations © individuals and organisations credited

All rights reserved. No part of this publication may be reproduced, stored in a retrieval system, or transmitted in any form or by any means, electronic, mechanical, photocopying, recording, or otherwise, without the prior permission of the copyright owner.

Publication Co-ordinator: Doug Ford
Book Design: Wayne Audrain
Image Collation: Julia Coutanche
Photography: Neil Mahrer and Gillian Carr unless credited